A l'office de tourisme

1	Qu'est-ce qu'on peut faire?	2
2	A l'office de tourisme	6
3	En ville	8
4	Directions	12
5	C'est loin?	14
6	C'est fermé!	16
7	Quel temps fait-il?	18
8	Au bureau de change	20
	Bande dessinée	22
	Entrée libre	24
	Vocabulaire	31

Julia Batters · Anneli McLachlan

1 Qu'est-ce qu'on peut faire?

In this unit you will learn how to:

- give details about things to do in your area
- say what your area is like
- ask about things to do.

1 On peut . . .

écoutez! Write down 1–8. Where can you go?
Listen to the tape.
Now add the letter of the place or places each person is told.

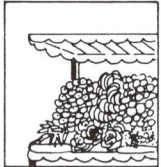
a

b

c

d

e

f

g

h

2 Et aussi on peut . . .

écoutez! Write down 1–4. What can you do in these four places?
Listen to the tape.
Now add the letter or letters of the thing or things each person is told.

a

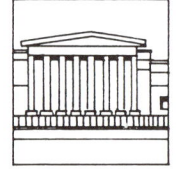
b

c

d

e

f

g

h

QU'EST-CE QU'ON PEUT FAIRE?

3 Quelle ville?

écoutez! Write down 1–6.
Which town is being described?
Listen to the tape. Now add the letter of the right town.

a **York**   b **Brighton**

c **London**    d **Edinburgh**

e **Exeter**   f **Norwich**

4 York

écoutez! Write down 1–6.
What is being said about York in this slide show for French visitors?
Look at the pictures below.
Listen to the tape. Now write down the letters of the right pictures.

a

b

c

d

e

f

QU'EST-CE QU'ON PEUT FAIRE?

5 A vous!

parlez! Can you remember how to tell French visitors what there is to do in a town?

Tell a French visitor that he or she can do these things.

go to shops   visit museum   go to beach   play tennis

6 Rappel!

parlez! Can you remember how to ask what there is to do?
If you need help, listen again to the tape for activity 1.

7 Allez-y!

parlez! Work with a partner.

One of you asks what there is to do.   The other answers.

 London?

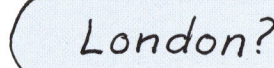 Brighton?

Norwich?

Liverpool?

Changez de rôle!

8 Ma ville (1)

parlez! What can you say about your town or area? Collect some pictures if you can. Work out sentences to go with each picture.
Make it sound as attractive as possible!

9 Ma ville (2)

 **écrivez!** Write out your sentences from activity 8 to send to a French-speaking friend.

QU'EST-CE QU'ON PEUT FAIRE?

10 Montréal, ville passionnante!

 **lisez!** Match the sentences from this brochure to the correct picture.

a

b

c

d

1 On peut visiter les musées et les monuments historiques.

2 On peut aller au théâtre et après au restaurant.

3 On peut faire des promenades, aller au parc.

4 On peut faire du shopping au centre-ville.

Now fill in your progress sheet ✓

Fini déjà? Tournez à la page 24.

mots clés

A

Qu'est-ce qu'on peut faire	à Birmingham? à Liverpool? dans le Kent?

B

A Birmingham A Liverpool Dans le Kent	on peut	aller	au marché. au parc. au centre sportif. au restaurant. au théâtre.
			en boîte.
			à la plage. à la piscine.
		visiter	les monuments historiques. les musées. les châteaux.
		faire	du shopping. des promenades. de l'équitation.
		jouer au tennis.	
C'est	une ville une région	très	calme. passionnante. charmante.

2 A l'office de tourisme

In this unit you will learn how to:

- deal with requests for information in a tourist office
- ask for information at a tourist office
- understand the key points in leaflets.

1 Une liste de . . .

écoutez! Write down 1–7. Which leaflet?
Listen to the tape.
Now add the letter of the leaflet each person wants.

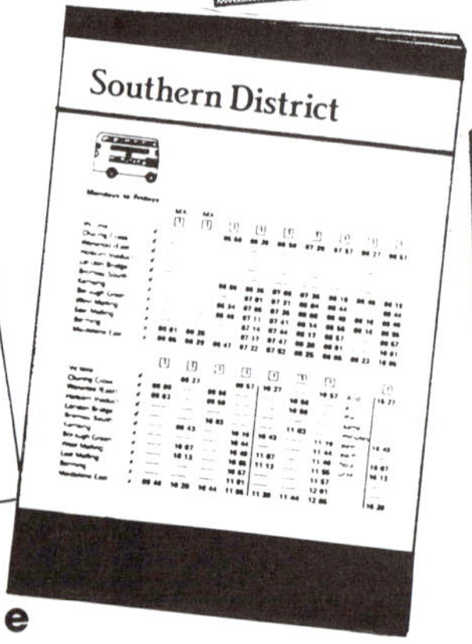

2 A vous!

parlez! Can you remember how to ask people if you can help them? Practise sounding as polite and helpful as you can!

A L'OFFICE DE TOURISME

3 Rappel!

parlez! Can you remember how to ask for different things?
Look back at activity 1. Ask for one of the leaflets.
Your partner points to the right leaflet to show he or she has understood.

4 Allez-y!

parlez! Work with a partner.
Make up conversations in a tourist office.

The tourist asks if the employee speaks French. The employee says yes and asks if he or she can help.

The tourist asks for the things shown and the employee responds politely.

Changez de rôle!

a

b

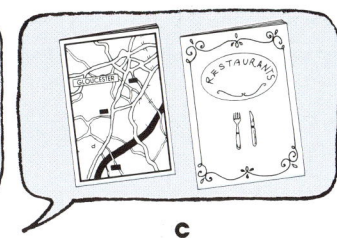
c

Now fill in your progress sheet ✓

Fini déjà? Tournez à la page 25.

mots clés

A

Excusez-moi	Madame. Monsieur.	Vous parlez français?
Avez-vous	une liste	de restaurants? d'hôtels? de campings? de visites en car? de monuments historiques?
	un dépliant sur les campings?	
	un plan de la ville?	
	un horaire	des bus?
		des trains?

B

Oui	Madame. Monsieur.	Je peux vous aider?
Voilà	Madame. Monsieur.	

3 En ville

In this unit you will learn how to:

- tell visitors where places in your town are
- ask for places in a town.

1 Voici...

écoutez! Write down 1–10. Which places are being pointed out?
Listen to the tape. Now add the letter of each place on the map.

2 Où se trouve...?

écoutez! Write down 1–9. Where do they want to go?
Listen to the tape. Now add the letter of the place each person wants.

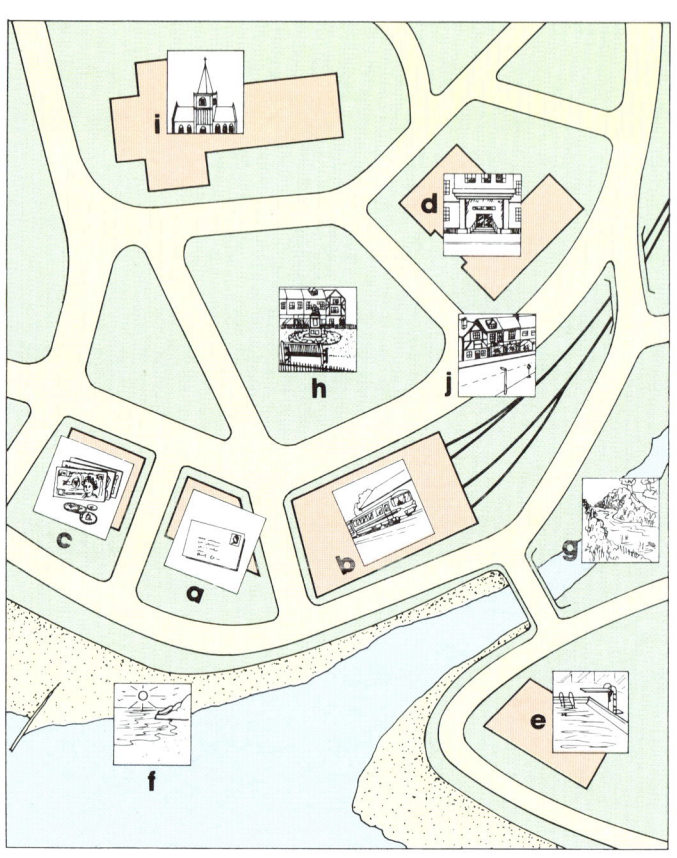

3 A vous!

parlez! Can you remember how to point out places in a town?
Look back at the pictures in activities 1 and 2 and test yourself or each other.

EN VILLE

4 En face

écoutez! Write down 1–8. Do these people give the right information? Look at the map. Listen to the tape. Now add a tick for true (✓) or a cross for false (✗).

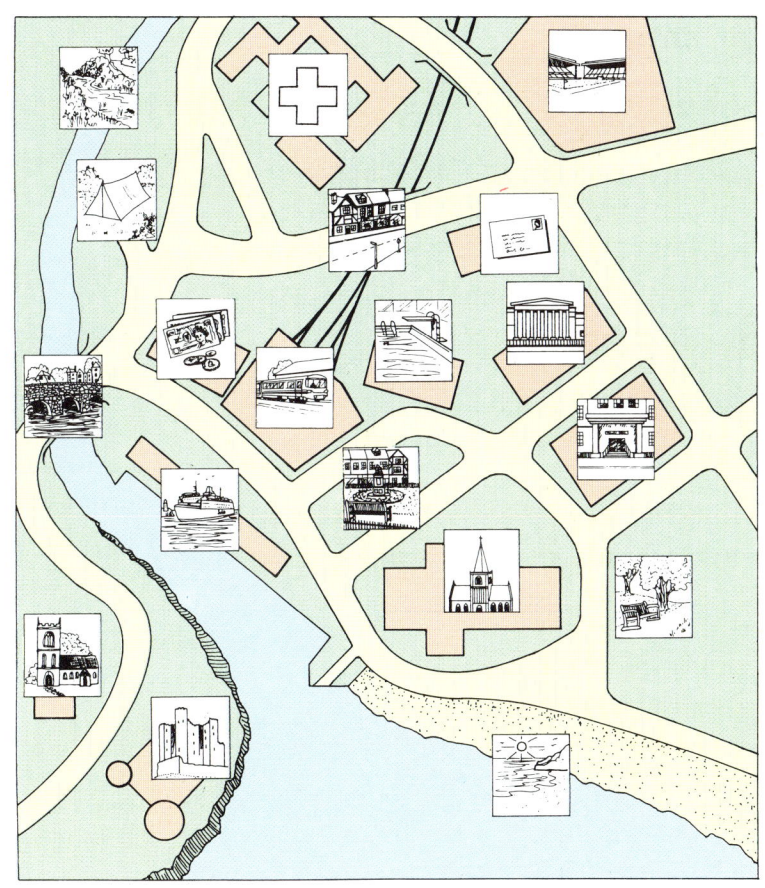

5 Où aller?

lisez! You're planning a guided tour for a group of French-speaking visitors.

They have sent this list of the places they would like to see.

Make a note of the places in English or draw a symbol for each place.

> la cathédrale
> le château
> l'église
> la rue principale
> le parc
> le musée

6 A vous!

parlez! Can you remember how to tell someone where something is?
Look back at the map in activity 4.
Using the map, say where the places in activity 5 are.

EN VILLE

7 Rappel!

 **parlez!** Can you remember how to ask where something is?

Look back at activity 4. Ask about one of the places.
Your partner points to the right symbol on the map to
show he or she has understood.

8 Allez-y!

 **parlez!** Work with a partner.

One of you asks for these places.

The other says where they are, using the map below.
You can give as much information as you like.

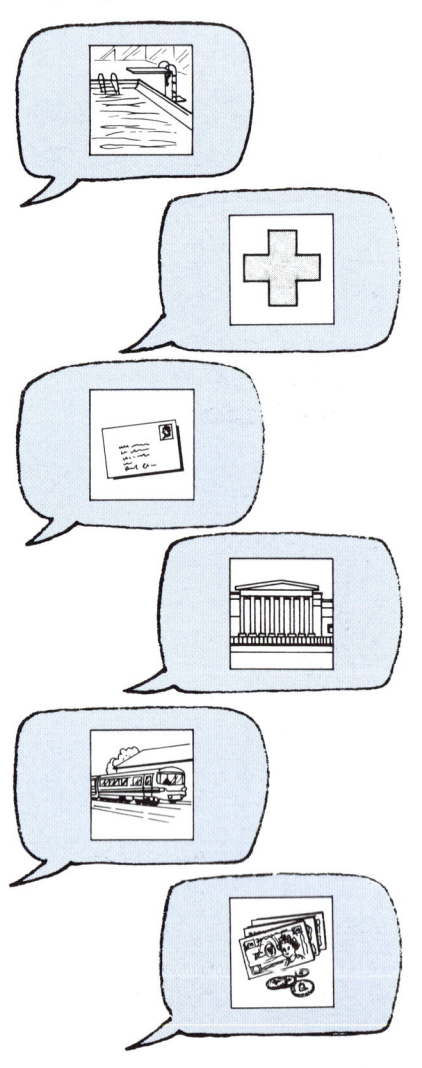

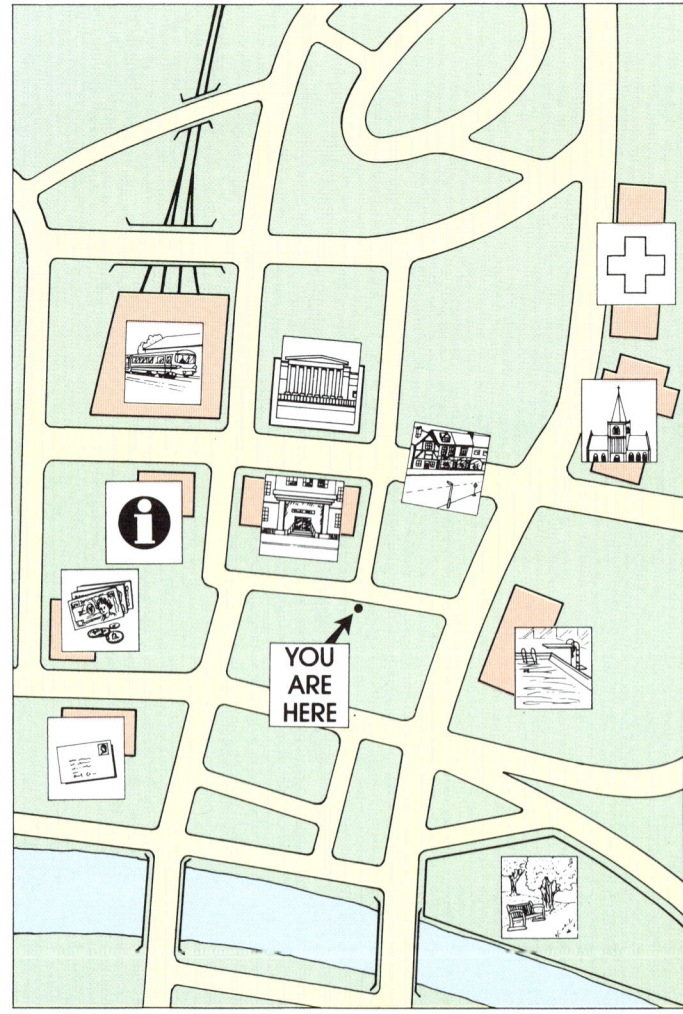

Changez de rôle!

EN VILLE

9 Un dépliant

**lisez!** Match the French words to the pictures.

1 le château de Raby
2 la rivière Tees
3 la cathédrale de Durham

a

c

b

mots clés

A

Où se trouve	la poste? la gare? la banque? la mairie? la piscine? la plage? la rivière? la place? la cathédrale? la rue principale?
	le camping? le château? le musée? le parc? le pont? le port? le stade?
	l'hôpital? l'église?

B

Voici	la poste. la gare. la banque. la mairie. la piscine. la plage. la rivière. la place. la cathédrale. la rue principale.	
	le camping. le château. le musée. le parc. le pont. le port. le stade.	
	l'hôpital. l'église.	
La poste se trouve	à côté	de la mairie. de la gare.
	près	
	en face	du parc. du stade.
		de l'hôpital.

Now fill in your progress sheet ✓

Fini déjà?
Tournez à la page 26.

4 Directions

In this unit you will learn how to:
- give directions to places in town
- ask for directions.

1 Tournez à gauche!

 écoutez! Write down 1–8. Which direction?
Listen to the tape.
Now add the letter of the directions given to each person.
If you like, add the place each visitor is asking for.

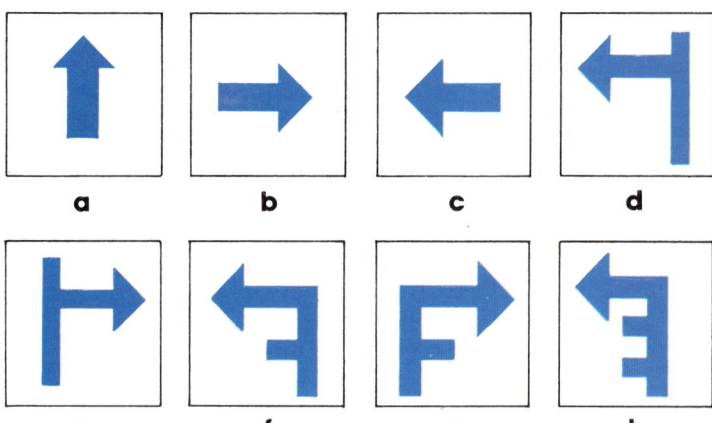

2 Au centre-ville

 écoutez! Write down 1–5. Are the directions correct?
Listen to the tape.
Now add whether the directions given are true (✓) or false (✗).

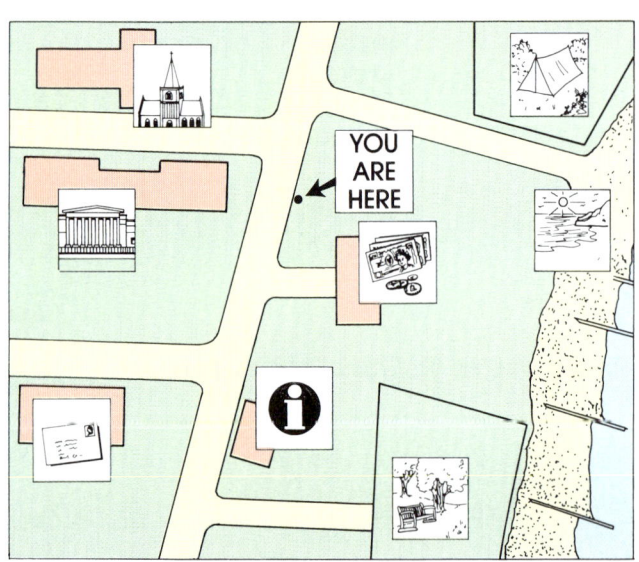

DIRECTIONS

3 A vous!

parlez! Can you remember how to give someone directions? Look back at the pictures in activity 1. Practise giving the directions shown.

4 Rappel!

parlez! Can you remember how to ask for places in the town? Look back at activity 2. Practise asking for some of the places on the map.

5 Allez-y!

parlez! Work with a partner.

One of you asks for these places in the town.
The other uses the map on page 12 to give directions.

a b c d e f

Changez de rôle!

Now fill in your progress sheet ✓

Fini déjà? Tournez à la page 27.

mots clés

A

Excusez-moi	Madame. Monsieur.	Vous parlez français?

Le marché, Le musée, Le château, La poste, La rue principale, La gare, L'office de tourisme,	s'il vous plaît?

Merci	Madame. Monsieur.

B

Oui.

Allez tout droit.			
Tournez	à gauche. à droite.		
Prenez la	première deuxième troisième	rue	à droite. à gauche.
De rien. Au revoir.			

13

5 C'est loin?

In this unit you will learn how to:

- say whether a place is near or far
- suggest the best way of getting there
- ask whether a place is near or far.

1 C'est loin?

 écoutez! a Write down 1–6.
Where do they want to go?
Listen to the tape. Now add the letter of the place each person wants.
Also add if the place is near (N) or far (F).

a b c d e f

b How to travel?
Listen to the tape again.
Now write down the letter of the means of transport suggested.

a b c d e

2 A vous!

 **parlez!** Can you remember how to tell someone whether a place is near or far?

Can you remember how to suggest a means of transport?
Look back at activity 1b and suggest each of the means of transport shown.

3 Rappel!

 parlez! Can you remember how to *ask* whether places are near or far?
Look back at activity 1a and ask about each of the pictures.

C'EST LOIN?

4 Allez-y!

 **parlez!** Work with a partner. Practise these conversations.

One of you plays the visitor.   The other responds.

a Ask if the station is near. — No.
b Ask if the beach is near. — No.
c Ask if the park is far. — No, it's near.

Changez de rôle!

5 Prenez le bus!

 **parlez!** Get a map of your own town. Practise asking where places are, saying whether they're near or far and suggesting the best way to get there.

Now fill in your progress sheet ✓

mots clés

A

Excusez-moi	Madame. Monsieur.	Vous parlez français?
Le parc, Le musée, La poste, La gare, La plage, Le stade,	c'est loin? c'est près?	
Merci.		

B

Oui.	
Oui, Non,	c'est loin. c'est près.
Prenez	le bus. le car. un taxi. le métro.
Vous pouvez y aller à pied.	
De rien. Au revoir.	

6 C'est fermé!

In this unit you will learn how to:

- tell people about opening and closing times

- ask about opening and closing times.

1 A quelle heure?

écoutez! Write down 1–6. What are the opening times? Listen to the tape. Now add the letter of the sign which matches.

a 9.30–12.00

b 11.00–15.00 closed Mondays

c 9.00–13.00 14.00–18.00

d 3pm–5.30pm every day

e 9.00–16.00 closed Sat & Sun

f 8–10 Mon Tues Wed

2 A vous!

parlez! Can you remember how to say what time a place is open or closed? Practise, using the signs in activity 1.

3 Rappel!

parlez! Can you remember how to ask when a place is open or closed?

 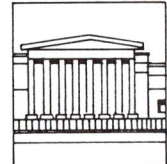 

4 Allez-y!

parlez! Work with a partner. One of you asks when the places on the right are open or closed. The other replies.

Changez de rôle!

5 Le lundi . . .

lisez! a Look at this sign from a shop in France. Make a note of when it is open.

écrivez! b Now write a sign for one of the places in activity 4.

Now fill in your progress sheet

Fini déjà? Tournez aux pages 28 et 29.

mots clés

A

La poste	Le château	ferme	à quelle heure?
La banque	Le musée	ouvre	
La piscine			

B

Le	lundi, mardi, mercredi, jeudi, vendredi, samedi, dimanche,	elle il	ouvre ferme	à...heures.

7 Quel temps fait-il?

In this unit you will learn how to:
- talk about the climate in your area
- ask about the climate.

1 Il fait beau

écoutez! **a** Write down 1–8.
What's the weather like today?
Listen to the tape.
Now add the letter of the weather talked about in each conversation.

a b c

d e f

g h

b Listen again and see if you can spot the words for 'in winter' and 'in summer'.

2 Vrai ou faux?

écoutez! Write down 1–6.
True or false?
Listen to the tape.
Look at the map.
Now add T (true) or F (false) for each statement.

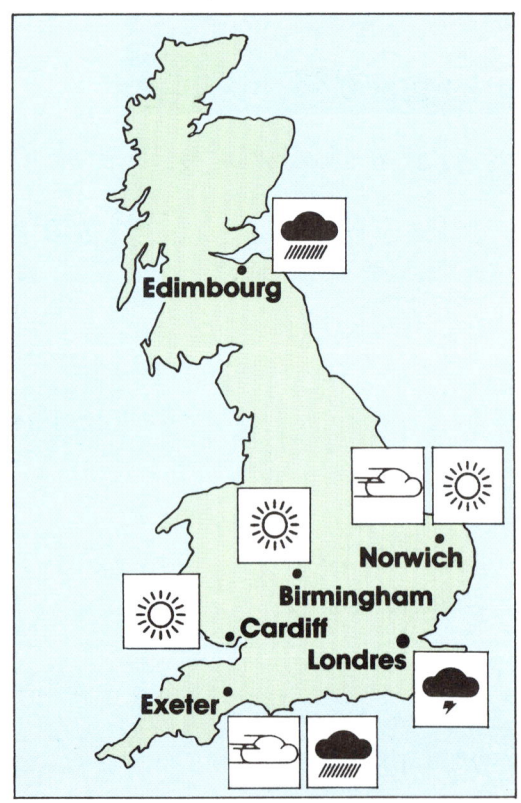

QUEL TEMPS FAIT-IL?

3 A vous!

 **parlez!** Can you remember how to say what the weather is like? Practise, using the pictures in activity 1 and the map in activity 2.

4 Rappel!

 **parlez!** Can you remember how to ask what the weather is like?

5 Allez-y!

 **parlez!** Work with a partner.

a Use the map on page 18.
One of you asks what the weather is like in summer in:
- Edinburgh
- London
- Birmingham
- Exeter
- Norwich
- Cardiff

The other says what the weather is like.

Changez de rôle!

b One of you is a French-speaking visitor. Here are the things you like to do.
- getting a sun tan
- winter sports.

Ask about the weather in summer and in winter.

The other is a tourist office employee. You want to encourage tourists to visit your region. How do you answer?

Changez de rôle!

mots clés

A

Quel temps fait-il à
Londres
Edimbourg
Birmingham
Exeter
Norwich
Cardiff
aujourd'hui?
en été?
en hiver?

B

Il fait	beau	(en été).
	mauvais	(en hiver).
	froid	(aujourd'hui).
	chaud	
	du soleil	
Il	neige	
	pleut	
	gèle	
Il y a	du vent	
	du brouillard	
	de l'orage	
C'est un climat	superbe.	
	agréable.	
	dur.	

Now fill in your progress sheet ✓

Fini déjà? Tournez à la page 30.

8 Au bureau de change

In this unit you will learn how to:

- change money for customers
- change money in a French-speaking country.

1 Change

écoutez! Write down 1–6. How much do they change?
Listen to the tape. Now add the letter of the amount each person wants to change.

a

b

c

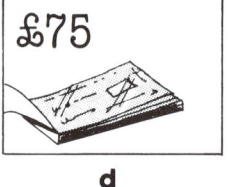

d

e

f

2 Identité

écoutez! Write down 1–4. What identification do they have?
Listen to the tape. Now add P for passport or C for identity card.

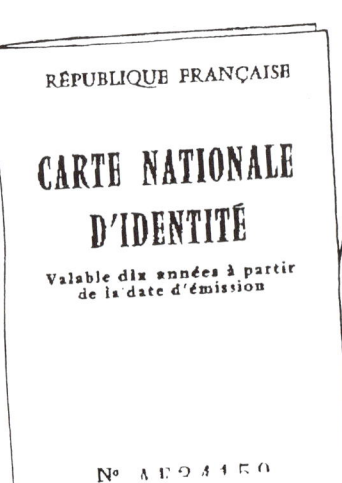

AU BUREAU DE CHANGE

3 A vous!

 Can you remember how to ask people:
- if you can help them?
- if they have identification?
- if they can sign?

Look at the mots-clés if you need help.

4 Rappel!

 Can you remember how to:
- say you want to change some money?
- say how much you want to change?
- offer identification?

Practise, using the pictures on page 20.

5 Allez-y!

 Work with a partner. One of you plays the employee.

Ask if you can help the customer.

Ask for identification.

Ask the customer to sign.

The other plays the customer. Say you want to change the following:

Changez de rôle!

mots clés

A

Je peux vous aider	Monsieur? Madame?
Bien sûr. Combien?	
Avez-vous une pièce d'identité?	
Voulez-vous signer ici?	

B

Je voudrais changer	de l'argent. des chèques de voyage.
(Je voudrais changer)	cinquante livres sterling. cinq cents francs français.
Oui, voilà	mon passeport. ma carte d'identité.
Bien sûr.	

Activités

1 Find the French for:

   a What can you do at Waterville?
   b You can go for walks.
   c Thank you. Goodbye!
   d You can go horse riding.
   e Of course. Here you are sir.

2 Unjumble these words from the story.

   a NEDSAMOPER   b ITSEL
   c UNERJOE   d AUBUPEOC

3 The tourist office assistant didn't get the chance to say everything that could be done in her town.

   Look at the posters in the story and work out what else she could have said.

4 Write another story by changing any details you like.

Qu'est-ce qu'on peut faire?

1 Boulogne

 **lisez!** The tourist office in Boulogne has given you this leaflet.
You are in Boulogne for a week.
Make a list of something that you and your friend can do every day.

LOISIRS
ACADÉMIE DE BILLARD
69, rue de Paris - Le Touquet - 21.05.00.58
Salle de billards français de compétition, snooker, pétanque billard
BATEAU
Espadon Club - 21.30.34.38
BIBLIOTHÈQUE
Les Annonciades, place du Palais de Justice - 21.80.46.52
Du mardi au samedi de 14 h à 18 h et mercredi/samedi 9 h à 12 h
CHEVAL
Club Hippique du Boulonnais, route de Conteville, La Capelle
21.83.32.38
Centre Equestre de la Ferme des Rietz
Lieu-dit Herquelingue - Isques - 21.31.22.06
GOLF
Hardelot : 21.83.73.10
Wimereux : 21.32.43.20
Le Touquet : Le Manoir - 21.05.20.22
PÊCHE EN MER
Sorties en mer - 21.31.94.10
PISCINES
Route du Portel, Outreau - 21.31.70.85
Piscine municipale, centre national de la mer - 21.30.78.30
Ouverte au public
En période scolaire :
mardi et vendredi de 12 h à 14 h et de 17 h 30 à 20 h
mercredi, samedi et dimanche de 10 h à 17 h, le jeudi de 12 h à 14 h
Durant les vacances scolaires :
mardi, mercredi, jeudi de 10 h à 19 h
vendredi de 10 h à 20 h, samedi et dimanche de 10 h à 17 h
Fermé le lundi
PORT DE PLAISANCE
Club House : 21.31.80.67
TENNIS
Boulevard Eurvin : 21. 80.46.02
Salle Waroquerie : 21.80.11.45

3 Dépliants

 **écrivez!** Make a leaflet showing what there is to do where you live.
Use the leaflets on this page to give you some ideas.
Look back at the mots-clés on page 5 for help.

2 Mauroux

 lisez! You are the leader of a group of British tourists in Mauroux.
You have made a note of their interests in your diary.
Will all your customers be happy in Mauroux?

> Mauroux:
> tennis   river
> walks   disco
> riding   bowling

MAUROUX
EN QUERCY

LOISIRS, DÉTENTE, SPORT, ANIMATIONS

- Sa rivière : Le LOT (canoë-kayak, pêche)
- Ses sentiers pédestres,
- Ses centres équestres,
- Son club de pétanque,
- Son tennis,
- Sa discothèque,
- Plans d'eau à proximité.

A l'office de tourisme

1 Les voyages

 lisez! You're helping to plan trips to France for groups of British and American tourists.
You have sent off for some leaflets.
You want to organize a special day for each group.
You have three groups of tourists.
Who will go to which place?

1 a group of farmers

2 a group of people who like fishing

3 a group of people interested in design and technology.

Jot down any useful details about each place.

a

b

c

2 Une lettre

 lisez! Someone has written to your tourist office from France. Here is part of his letter. What is he asking for? Which of the leaflets on page 6 will you send?

> Je vous serais très reconnaissant si vous pourriez m'envoyer les choses suivantes.
> – une liste de campings
> – une liste de restaurants
> – un plan de la ville
> – un dépliant sur les monuments historiques

En ville

1 Vous êtes interprète!

 lisez! Answer your English friends' questions about this leaflet.

Two guided tours are offered.
- What places are visited in each one?
- What days does the first one happen and what months of the year?
- What time does it start?
- Where should people meet?
- How long does it last?
- What is different about the second one?

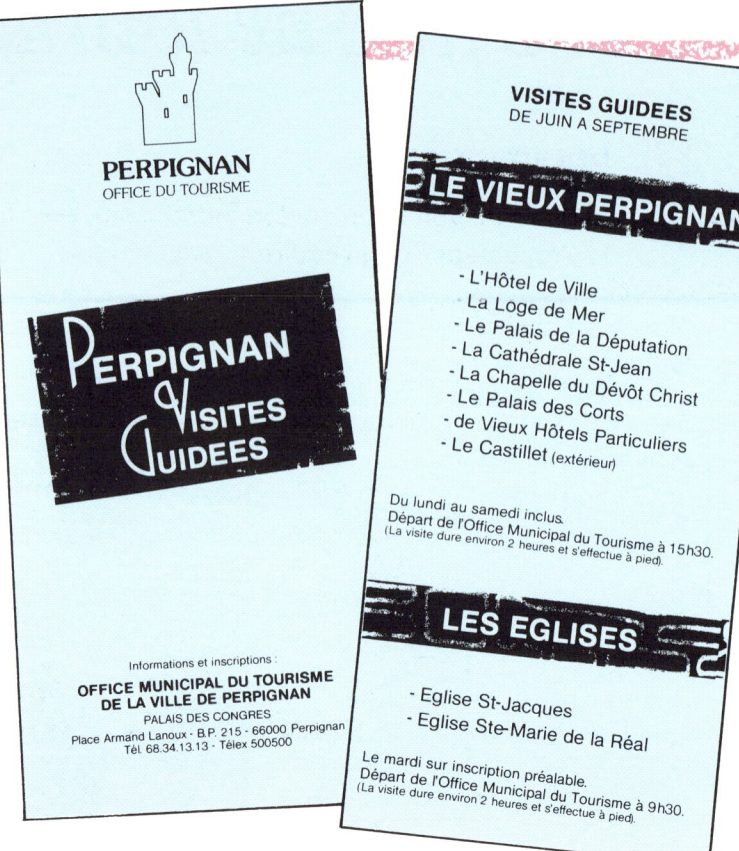

2 Vrai ou faux?

 **lisez!**
écrivez! You have written this note for some French-speaking tourists.

> Banque – à côté de la gare
> Musée – en face de la gare
> Camping – près de la rivière
> Mairie – en face du musée

Check the information against the map.
Is any of the information wrong?

Write the note out again. Correct any wrong information.

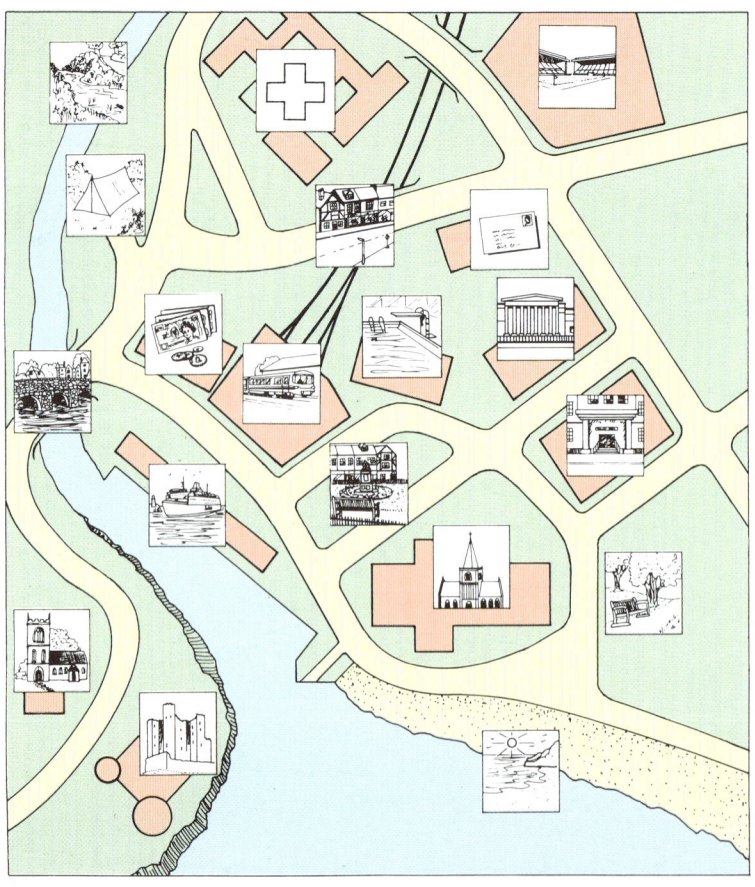

3 Ma ville

écrivez!
parlez!
dessinez!

Make up your own guided tour of your town for French-speaking visitors.

You could make:
- a map of the town with places labelled in French
- a taped commentary (in case you can't do the tour personally)
- a brochure advertising your tour (days, time, cost, starting place, etc.).

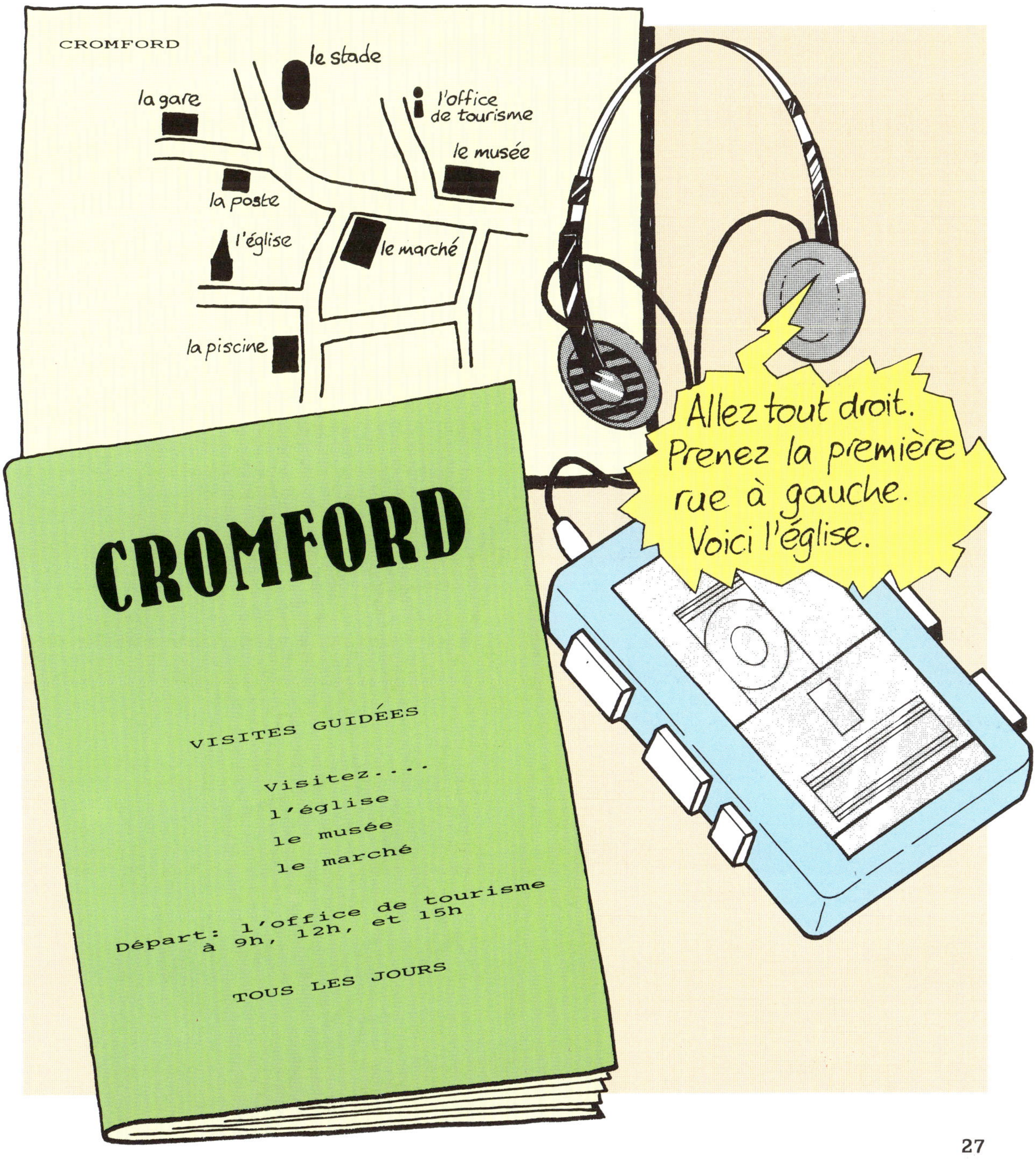

Allez tout droit. Prenez la première rue à gauche. Voici l'église.

CROMFORD

VISITES GUIDÉES

Visitez....
l'église
le musée
le marché

Départ: l'office de tourisme
à 9h, 12h, et 15h

TOUS LES JOURS

C'est fermé!

1 C'est ouvert?

lisez! When are these places open for visitors?

Jot down the details for a group of English-speaking tourists in France.

What do you think Parc Minifrance is?

a

L'ARC DE TRIOMPHE

Jean Feuillie C n m h s

PLACE DE L'ETOILE

Place de l'Etoile. 75008 Paris - Tél. : 43.80.31.31
Monument historique d'Etat / Ministère de la Culture.
Direction du Patrimoine.
Visite : De 10 h à 17 h 30 du 1er avril au 30 septembre.
De 10 h à 16 h 30 du 1er octobre au 31 mars.
- Panorama sur Paris, de la Plate-forme.
- Exposition de documents et audiovisuel *La légende de l'Arc*, en permanence dans la Grande Salle.

b

FRANCE — ARDÈCHE
Site Classé
AVEN-GROTTE DE LA FORESTIÈRE ★★★

NOUVEAU
Dans la Grotte, visitez le laboratoire d'acclimatation pour animaux et insectes cavernicoles !

HORAIRES
Ouvert tous les jours, de 10 h à 19 h des Rameaux au 20 septembre.

Pour les groupes toute l'année, sur rendez-vous par lettre.

PHOTO R. DELON
Sur la D217, entre Orgnac et Vallon Pont d'Arc

c

PARC MINIFRANCE
BRIGNOLES - FRANCE
UNIQUE EN FRANCE

OUVERT DE 9 H A 24 H
RESTAURATION PERMANENTE

LA FRANCE EN MINIATURE

C'EST FERMÉ

PROMENADES EN BATEAU

Au pied des Châteaux de BEYNAC - FAYRAC CASTELNAUD & MARQUEYSSAC

PROMENADE COMMENTEE
de 45 MINUTES
TOUS LES JOURS
de MAI à OCTOBRE

Départ de 10h à 19h
toutes les 30 Minutes,
du pied du Parking de Beynac.
(10Kms Sud-Ouest de Sarlat)

TARIFS

Adultes.............................	30 F
Enfants (jusqu'à 12 ans)......	15 F
Groupes (à partir de 20).......	25 F

Billets sur place

Réservation
(Pour groupes seulement)

2 Promenades en bateau

 lisez!   Look at this leaflet.

- How long does the boat trip last?
- What time of year can you go?
- What time does the boat leave?
- How much does it cost?

3 Entrée

 lisez!   Where is this ticket for?
Did the person pay the full price?

4 Préhisto

 lisez!   What kind of museum are these tickets for?
How much did they cost?

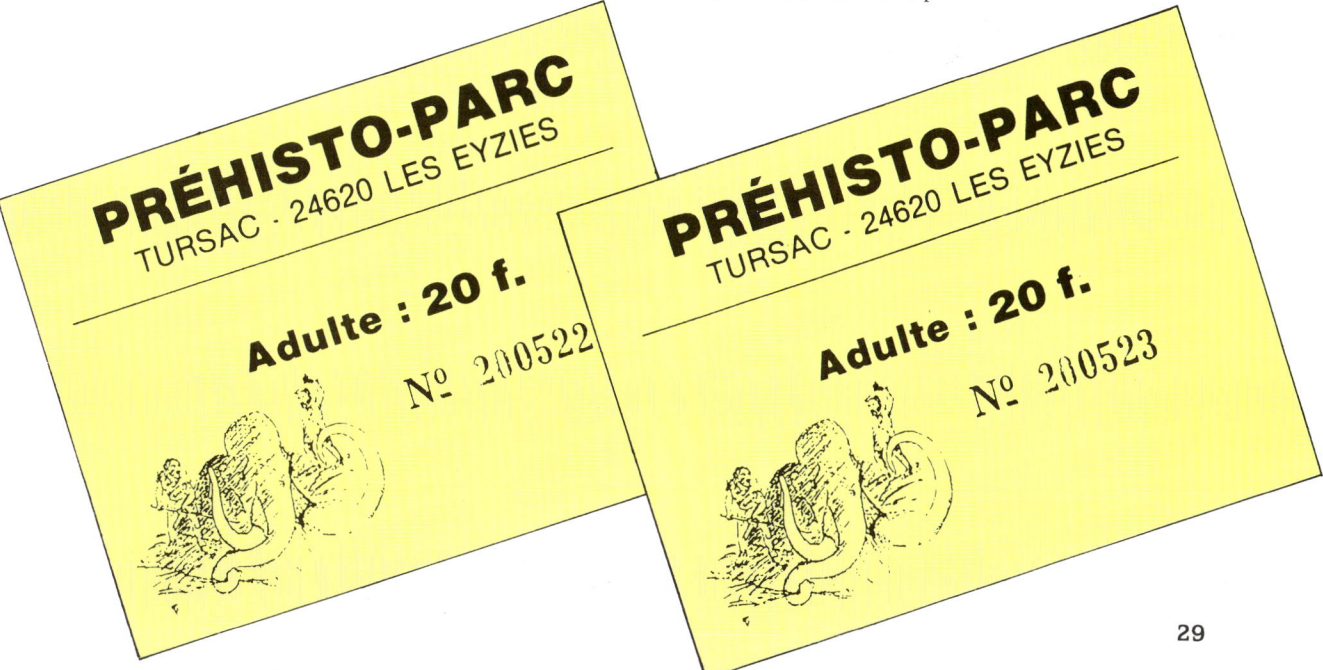

Quel temps fait-il?

1 Météo

lisez! What does this advertise?
What number do you have to ring?
How much does it cost?

2 Une carte

lisez! You are about to take a group of young skiers to St. Moritz.

You have just received this message.
It's from the ski instructor in Switzerland.
What does she tell you?

> Il fait très, très beau à St Moritz. Pendant la journée il fait du soleil et il fait assez chaud. La nuit il neige — c'est superbe!

3 Il fait . . .

écrivez! What would the instructor have written if the weather had been foggy and cold?

Vocabulaire

Unit 1

qu'est-ce qu'on peut faire? what can you do?
on peut aller . . . you can go . . .

au marché to the market
au parc to the park
au centre sportif to the sports centre
au restaurant to the restaurant
au théâtre to the theatre
en boîte to the disco
à la plage to the beach
à la piscine to the swimming pool

visiter visit
les monuments historiques historic buildings
les musées museums
les châteaux castles

faire du shopping go shopping
faire des promenades go for walks
faire de l'équitation go horse riding

jouer au tennis play tennis

Unit 2

excusez-moi excuse me
vous parlez français? do you speak French?
avez-vous . . . ? do you have . . . ?

une liste de restaurants a list of restaurants
hôtels hotels
campings campsites
visites en car coach tours
monuments historiques historic buildings
un dépliant sur les campings a leaflet about campsites
un plan de la ville a town plan
un horaire des bus a bus timetable
un horaire des trains a train timetable
je peux vous aider? can I help you?
voilà here you are

Unit 3

où se trouve? where is?
voici here is
en face de opposite
à côté de next to
près de near

la poste the post office
la gare the station
la banque the bank
la mairie the town hall
la piscine the swimming pool
la plage the beach
la rivière the river
la place the town square
la cathédrale the cathedral
la rue principale the main street
le camping the campsite
le château the castle
le musée the museum
le parc the park
le pont the bridge
le port the port
le stade the stadium
l'hôpital the hospital
l'église the church

Unit 4

excusez-moi excuse me
vous parlez français? do you speak French?

le marché the market
le musée the museum
le château the castle
la poste the post office
la rue principale the main street
la gare the station
l'office de tourisme the tourist office

allez tout droit go straight on
tournez à gauche turn left
tournez à droite turn right
prenez la première rue à droite take the first road on the right
la deuxième the second
la troisième the third
de rien you're welcome
au revoir goodbye

Unit 5

excusez-moi excuse me
vous parlez français? do you speak French?
c'est loin? is it far?
c'est près? is it near?
c'est loin it is far
c'est près it's nearby

VOCABULAIRE

le parc the park
le musée the museum
la poste the post office
la gare the station
la plage the beach
le stade the stadium

prenez le bus take the bus
le car the coach
un taxi a taxi
le métro the underground

vous pouvez y aller à pied go there on foot
de rien you're welcome
au revoir goodbye

Unit 6

. . . ouvre à quelle heure? what time does . . . open?
. . . ferme à quelle heure? what time does . . . close?

la poste the post office
la banque the bank
la piscine the swimming pool
le musée the museum
le château the castle

lundi Monday
mardi Tuesday
mercredi Wednesday
jeudi Thursday
vendredi Friday
samedi Saturday
dimanche Sunday
il/elle ferme à . . . heures it closes at . . . o'clock
il/elle ouvre à . . . heures it opens at . . . o'clock

Unit 7

quel temps fait-il? what is the weather like?
aujourd'hui today
en été in summer
en hiver in winter

il fait beau it's nice
il fait mauvais it's nasty
il fait froid it's cold
il fait chaud it's hot
il fait du soleil it's sunny

il neige it's snowing/it snows
il pleut it's raining/it rains
il gèle it's freezing

il y a du vent it's windy
il y a du brouillard it's foggy
il y a de l'orage it's stormy
c'est un climat superbe the climate is superb
agréable pleasant
dur harsh

Unit 8

je peux vous aider? can I help you?
je voudrais . . . I would like . . .
changer to change

de l'argent some money
des chèques de voyage some travellers' cheques

bien sûr certainly
combien? how much?

cinquante fifty
cinq cents five hundred

livres sterling English pounds
francs français French francs
avez-vous . . . ? do you have . . . ?
une pièce d'identité some identification
voilà here is
mon passeport my passport
ma carte d'identité my identity card